THANKSGIVING

JOKES

UNCLE AMON

www.UncleAmon.com

ISBN: 9781973143970

TABLE OF CONTENTS

Funny Thanksgiving Jokes

Q: WHY DID THE TURKEY CROSS THE ROAD?

A: HE HAD TO PROVE THAT HE WASN'T A CHICKEN!

Q: WHERE DID THE PILGRIMS LAND WHEN THEY CAME TO AMERICA?

A: ON THEIR FEET!

Q: WHO IS NEVER HUNGRY ON THANKSGIVING?

A: A TURKEY BECAUSE IT IS ALWAYS STUFFED!

Q: WHAT WAS THE PILGRIM'S FAVORITE DANCE?

A: THE PLYMOUTH ROCK!

Q: WHAT DO VAMPIRES PUT ON MASHED POTATOES?

A: GRAVE-Y!

Q: WHAT DID THE TURKEY SAY TO THE HUNTER?

A: QUACK! QUACK!

Q: WHY DID THE PILGRIMS WANT TO COME TO AMERICA DURING THE SPRING?

A: APRIL SHOWERS BRING MAY FLOWERS!

Q: WHY DID THE HUNTER SHOOT THE TURKEY?

A: HE WAS IN A FOWL MOOD!

Q: WHICH COUNTRY DOES NOT CELEBRATE THANKSGIVING?

A: TURKEY!

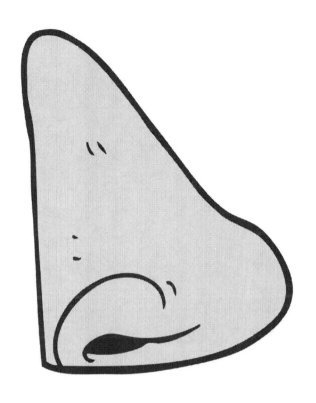

Q: WHAT SMELLS SO GOOD AT THANKSGIVING?

A: YOUR NOSE!

Q: WHAT DO YOU GET WHEN YOU CROSS A TURKEY WITH AN OCTOPUS?

A: ENOUGH DRUMSTICKS TO FEED THE ENTIRE NEIGHBORHOOD!

Q: WHAT DID THE ARMY GENERAL DO ON THANKSGIVING?

A: HE GAVE TANKS!

Q: WHAT DID THE SNOWMAN EAT ON THANKSGIVING?

A: AN ICE-BURGER!

Q: HOW DO YOU STUFF A TURKEY?

A: BUY HIM SOME PIZZA AND CHEESEBURGERS!

Q: WHY DID THE MONSTER GET FINED ON THANKSGIVING?

A: HE EXCEEDED THE FEED LIMIT!

Q: WHAT BIRD HAS WINGS BUT CANNOT FLY?

A: A ROASTED TURKEY!

Q: WHAT PART OF A TURKEY HAS THE MOST FEATHERS?

A: THE OUTSIDE!

Q: HOW DO YOU KNOW THE INDIANS WERE THE FIRST PEOPLE IN NORTH AMERICA?

A: THEY HAD RESERVATIONS!

Q: WHY WAS THE THANKSGIVING SOUP SO EXPENSIVE?

A: IT WAS MADE OF 24 CARROTS!

Q: WHAT DID THE MONSTER SAY TO THE THANKSGIVING TURKEY?

A: I AM PLEASED TO EAT YOU!

Q: WHAT IS BROWN AND WHITE AND FLIES ALL OVER?

A: A THANKSGIVING TURKEY BEING CARVED WITH A CHAIN SAW!

Q: WHY DID THE PILGRIMS FIRST EAT TURKEY ON THANKSGIVING?

A: THEY COULD NOT FIT A MOOSE IN THE OVEN!

Q: WHY DID THE PILGRIM'S PANTS KEEP FALLING DOWN?

A: THEY WORE THEIR BELT BUCKLES ON THEIR HAT!

Q: WHY WAS THANKSGIVING INVENTED?

A: ANOTHER EXCUSE TO WATCH FOOTBALL!

Q: WHY WAS THE TURKEY THROWN IN JAIL?

A: HE WAS SUSPECTED OF FOWL PLAY!

Q: WHAT IS BLACK AND WHITE AND RED ALL OVER?

A: A PILGRIM WITH POISON IVY!

Q: DID YOU HEAR ABOUT THE CRAZY TURKEY?

A: HE WAS READY FOR THANKSGIVING!

Q: WHY DIDN'T DAD GET A SECOND HELPING OF PIE?

A: BECAUSE HE ATE IT ALL THE FIRST TIME!

Q: WHAT DO YOU GET WHEN YOU CROSS A THANKSGIVING DESSERT AND A MONSTER?

A: BUMPKIN PIE!

Q: WHAT IS A TURKEY'S FAVORITE DESSERT?

A: CHERRY GOBBLER!

Q: CAN YOU SPELL INDIAN HOUSE WITH ONLY TWO LETTERS?

A: TP!

Q: HOW DOES THANKSGIVING ALWAYS END?

A: WITH THE LETTER G!

Q: WHAT IS A PUMPKIN'S FAVORITE GAME?

A: SQUASH!

Q: WHAT IS PURPLE AND BLUE AND HAS A LOT OF FEATHERS?

A: A TURKEY HOLDING ITS BREATH!

Q: WHAT IS THE BEST THING TO PUT IN A PECAN PIE?

A: YOUR TEETH!

Q: WHAT KIND OF KEY CANNOT UNLOCK A DOOR?

A: A TURKEY!

MAZE 1

MAZE 2

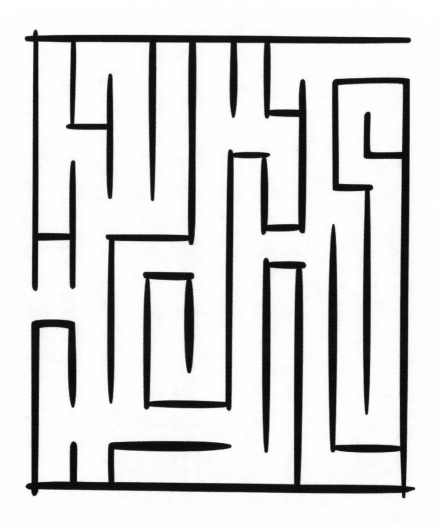

MAZE 3

MAZE 4

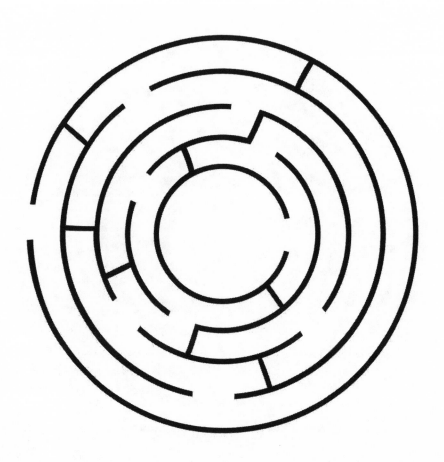

SOLUTIONS

ABOUT THE AUTHOR

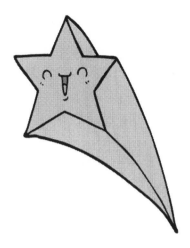

Uncle Amon began his career with a vision. It was to influence and create a positive change in the world through children's books by sharing fun and inspiring stories.

Whether it is an important lesson or just creating laughs, Uncle Amon provides insightful stories that are sure to bring a smile to your face! His unique style and creativity stand out from other children's book authors, because he uses real life experiences to tell a tale of imagination and adventure.

"I always shoot for the moon. And if I miss? I'll land in the stars." -Uncle Amon

For more fun books by Uncle Amon, please visit:

www.UncleAmon.com/books

Made in the USA
Middletown, DE
13 November 2020